# Foreword

Owning rabbits can be incredibly rewarding and a great source of companionship. Pets can provide opportunities for social interactions, helping people feel less lonely and isolated. Growing up with pets also offers health benefits, and caring for an animal can help improve a child's social skills, encouraging the development of compassion, understanding and a respect for living things. Having rabbits is, however, a huge responsibility and requires long-term commitment in terms of care and finances.

Before getting rabbits, it is important that time is taken to discuss the commitment and care required with all family members, and that everyone agrees to having and looking after rabbits. Bear in mind that once you have your rabbits there is a legal requirement under the Animal Welfare Act 2006 to care for them properly, so you must be sure that you will be able to do this throughout your rabbits' life. This means providing somewhere suitable for them to live, a healthy diet, opportunities to behave normally, the provision of appropriate company, and ensuring that they are well.

If you are able to care for rabbits properly and make the decision to go ahead, then please consider giving a home to some of the many rabbits currently in the RSPCA's animal centres throughout England and Wales.

This book is based on up-to-date knowledge of rabbit behaviour and welfare approved by the RSPCA. It has been written to provide you with all the care information you need to keep your rabbits happy and healthy throughout your lives together. We hope you enjoy it.

Samantha Gaines BSc (Hons) MSc PhD
Alice Potter BSc (Hons) MSc
Lisa Richards BSc (Hons)
Jane Tyson BSc (Hons) MSc PhD
Animal behaviour and welfare experts, Companion
Animals Department, RSPCA

# Introduction

Owning and caring for a pair or group of rabbits can be very rewarding. It is also a big responsibility and a long-term commitment. You will need to think carefully about lots of different things before you decide whether you are able to give rabbits the care and attention they need. Here are some of the issues you need to consider:

## Rabbits have complex needs

The biology and behaviour of pet rabbits is very similar to those of wild rabbits. This means they have very complex needs and although they are traditionally thought of as good pets for children, rabbits are not easy to look after well, so an adult must always be responsible for ensuring the rabbits are properly handled and cared for. Think very carefully about whether keeping rabbits fits in with your lifestyle. You will need to make sure that you can meet all their welfare needs – this includes providing suitable accommodation that is cleaned regularly, feeding them every day, as well as spending time grooming and interacting with them.

## Rabbits are a long-term commitment

Typically, rabbits may live for 8–12 years, although some may live longer. Think whether you can afford the costs of feeding and caring for rabbits. You will need to consider meeting the expense of a suitably robust, spacious home for them, food and bedding, equipment, vet bills and insurance. There may also be additional costs if you need to pay to board them or have them cared for when you go on holiday. Remember, too, that rabbits should always be kept in pairs or groups unless advised otherwise by a vet, so the costs will need to be multiplied by the number of rabbits you plan to keep.

## Rabbits are very sociable animals

This means that, as stated above, they must not be kept on their own – unless a vet or qualified animal behaviourist has advised you otherwise. A good mix is a male and female who have both been neutered. Rabbits should not be kept with other animals, such as guinea pigs.

## Rabbits are very active animals

They need plenty of space to hop, run, jump, dig and stretch out fully in any direction when lying down. They need an enclosure tall enough to allow them to stand up on their hind limbs without their ears touching the roof. A traditional hutch will not meet their needs, so you

should make sure you have enough room for a suitable house that has permanent access to an exercise area.

## The Animal Welfare Act

Under the Animal Welfare Act 2006 it is a legal obligation to care for animals properly by meeting five welfare

needs. These are: a suitable place to live, a healthy diet including clean, fresh water, the ability to behave normally, appropriate company and protection from pain, suffering, injury and illness. This care guide contains lots of information and tips to help you make sure these needs are met.

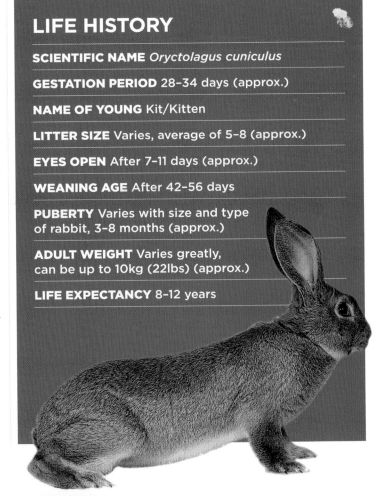

## LIFE HISTORY

**SCIENTIFIC NAME** *Oryctolagus cuniculus*

**GESTATION PERIOD** 28–34 days (approx.)

**NAME OF YOUNG** Kit/Kitten

**LITTER SIZE** Varies, average of 5–8 (approx.)

**EYES OPEN** After 7–11 days (approx.)

**WEANING AGE** After 42–56 days

**PUBERTY** Varies with size and type of rabbit, 3–8 months (approx.)

**ADULT WEIGHT** Varies greatly, can be up to 10kg (22lbs) (approx.)

**LIFE EXPECTANCY** 8–12 years

Make sure the type of rabbit you choose will suit your family and lifestyle.

# Choosing the right type of rabbits for you

If you are certain that you will be able to care for rabbits, the next stage is to do plenty of research to decide which type of rabbit is right for you.

## Age

If you have decided that baby rabbits, or kits, are suitable for your family and lifestyle, you will need to make sure that as well as being happy and healthy they have been weaned and are ready to leave their mother. Usually this time is from around 8 weeks old, but it varies from animal to animal.

## Sex

Rabbits are naturally sociable and should be kept in pairs or in a group unless your vet advises otherwise. A good combination is a male and female who have both been neutered. Rabbits can also be kept in same-sex pairs; the risk of fighting is reduced if they come from the same litter or are introduced to each other before 12 weeks of age. RSPCA centres will often have bonded pairs that need adopting. Whichever combination of rabbits you choose, it is advisable to get them neutered. This reduces the likelihood of fighting in both male and female rabbits and can have numerous health benefits, as well as minimizing the risk of unwanted pregnancies. Speak to your vet for detailed advice on neutering and when to do it.

## Size

Rabbits vary greatly in size, so this is an important consideration when you are thinking about which type to get. All rabbits need plenty of space, but bigger rabbits need larger accommodation. Think very carefully, therefore, about whether you have the space they need to be happy and healthy. If you are looking at a litter of kits, it is easy to overlook how big the rabbits may eventually become. A general guide to types of rabbit, with examples, can be found on the next page.

## Purebred or crossbreed

Whether you decide to buy purebred rabbits (the rabbit's parents are both the same single breed) or crossbreed (a mix of two or more breeds), there is

a huge variety to choose from. There are advantages to both purebreds and crossbreeds, and your decision may depend upon your personal preference and situation, and the circumstances of the rabbits you are considering. When purchasing purebred rabbits you will have a better idea of their parentage and what to expect in terms of their adult appearance. On the other hand, crossbreeds are less likely to show the exaggerated physical features and inherited diseases that are present in particular breeds, although they can still inherit disorders from their parents' breeds. They also generally cost less to buy.

Whatever type of rabbit you are thinking of getting, it is important to find out what health and physical issues they may be vulnerable to developing. As well as causing pain and suffering to your rabbits, such propensities may also lead to expensive bills for veterinary treatment. Knowing which types of rabbit tend to have fewer problems will give you the best chance of getting happy, healthy pets.

ABOVE: Knowing which breeds of rabbit have fewer problems will give you the best chance of choosing happy, healthy pets.

# Types of rabbit

For centuries, rabbits have been kept for their fur and meat, and more recently they have been kept as pets and for showing. Rabbits come in all shapes and sizes, with different-coloured coats and types of fur, which means that some people may like a particular type because of their looks. Keep in mind, however, that you must look beyond these generalizations, as every rabbit has their own unique character and temperament. The way they behave will depend upon how they are reared, cared for and treated.

Generally, rabbits fall into four types. Fur types have coats that are the most similar to the wild rabbit; the Rex tends to have shorter, smoother fur; lops have ears that hang down; while fancy types have been bred for unusual fur patterns, length or type of coat. It is important to remember that, regardless of the type of rabbit you choose, they all need appropriate care, company and a suitable diet and environment.

## Fur

The normal fur types have short, soft underhair interspersed with longer, stiffer guard hairs. Some rabbits of this type, such as the Silver Fox and the Chinchilla, have fur similar to that of the animals after which they are named. Other normal fur breeds include the Argentes, Beverens, New Zealand and Siberians – most of which come in several colours, such as blue, black, white or cream.

## Rex

The Rex is a 20th-century breed. Rex rabbits are characterized by short, dense fur that looks and

**TOP TIP**

Whatever type of rabbits you choose, remember that they should not be kept with other animals, such as guinea pigs, because their needs and diet are completely different.

feels like plush. Rexes are bred in a range of colours and are crossed with many of the other rabbit breeds to produce, for instance, the Chinchilla Rex. Some rabbits of this crossbreed type, such as the Astrex, have curly coats.

## Lop

Lops are bred in a range of colours and sizes, but all of them have ears that are floppy and hang down. Examples include French and German lops. Lop-eared rabbits can suffer from dental problems and ear infections because of their exaggerated features.

## Fancy

Decades of breeding have produced variations in the coat textures and patterns of some rabbits, as well as their ears and overall size. Some types, such as Dutch, English and Himalayan rabbits, have distinctive patterns to their fur that are not found in wild rabbits. English rabbits usually have white coats with a pattern in blue, black, tortoiseshell, chocolate or grey. The Dutch is a bi- or tri-coloured rabbit with fur that appears in a range of colours – including tortoiseshell, chocolate, yellow, blue and grey on a

white background. Some fancy types, such as the Himalayan, are smaller than average, while others, such as Flemish Giants and Harlequin, are much larger than average.

Angoras are sometimes kept for their wool. Remember, though, that if you are thinking of getting Angoras you will need to make sure that you have enough time each day to carefully groom their long hair to keep it in good condition.

LEFT TO RIGHT: Chinchilla, Rex Dalmatian, Lop-eared rabbit, Magpie Rex.

LEFT: This rabbit at the RSPCA Animal Centre in South Godstone is just one of the many animals waiting to be rehomed.
ABOVE: Make sure that the rabbits you buy are healthy.

# Buying rabbits

## Where to buy

Although you may have decided which size and type of rabbit is most suitable for your family, you should take your time in selecting the right individual rabbits.

The RSPCA encourages anyone looking for rabbits to consider offering some of the thousands it rescues each year a good home. Rehoming charities such as the RSPCA often have kits as well as adult rabbits for rehoming. They may have both crossbreed and purebred rabbits of all shapes and sizes available, and they may also have bonded pairs that are looking for a home.

If you buy your rabbits directly from the person who bred them, do some research first to make sure that you choose a responsible breeder. Breeders should be happy to discuss with you subjects such as how the kits have been kept. It is important, wherever possible, to see the kits with their mothers as this will give you a good picture of how well they have been cared for and their eventual size and sociability.

Avoid advertisements that invite you to meet the breeder to collect kits any place other than where the kits were born. You will be unable to see where the kits have come from, as well as the behaviour and health of the parents.

If you are going to buy a rabbit from a pet shop, only buy from outlets that meet all the welfare needs of animals in their care and also ensure that this information is freely available for potential owners.

## Meeting rabbits

Before you go to see a breeder, it is a good idea to call first. A good breeder will be happy to talk to you and answer any questions you may have. When you visit, look for signs that the litter (and parents) seem healthy and well cared for. If the rabbits seem nervous or timid, they may not have had enough chances to socialize and this could mean that they will be scared or anxious as they grow older and won't enjoy being handled. If you feel that anything is not quite right about the situation it is best to walk away and choose your rabbits from someone else.

## Information

A reputable breeder should supply you with notes about how to care for your new rabbits. This should include information about how they have been looked after thus far. It is particularly important to find out about their diet and, in particular, what type of foods they are used to, as well as checking if they have been vaccinated or microchipped (for more on vaccinations and microchipping, see pages 40–1). Ideally a breeder should provide you with a week's food for each rabbit, too, as any sudden changes to their diet could make them very ill. Speak to your vet for further detailed advice on how to feed young rabbits.

## Finding healthy rabbits

Wherever you view your rabbits, you should always check that they are healthy. Here are some signs that might indicate a rabbit has an underlying medical problem:

- Not eating or drinking
- A swollen abdomen
- Being under- or overweight
- Wounds or sores on the skin
- Signs of external parasites (e.g. fleas), such as scratching, areas of hair loss
- Staining, sores or signs of diarrhoea around the tail or bottom; dirty or matted fur
- Overgrown or damaged claws
- Dirty ears
- Weakness, wobbliness or difficulty standing up; lethargy
- Noisy or laboured breathing
- Overgrown, dirty, uneven or misaligned teeth
- Runny nose or sneezing
- Crusty or runny eyes, dull-looking eyes
- Fur loss, sores on the feet or hocks, cysts between toes

These are just a few examples. If you notice anything at all that doesn't look quite right with the rabbits you have seen, you may want to consider getting your rabbits from somewhere else. If you have concerns about the welfare of any of the animals you have visited, call the RSPCA (details can be found at www.rspca.org.uk).

# Biology

## Exaggerated features

Some breeds have been bred to emphasize certain physical features that, over time, have become more and more exaggerated. Although these features may be 'normal' for a specific breed, small heads and lop ears are just a few examples of breed features that may cause problems to the animal's health. Other breeds can be particularly prone to inherited disorders and diseases. Some of these issues will result in lifelong health problems and suffering. Try to ensure that any rabbits you choose are free from any exaggerated features.

## Ears

In the wild, a rabbit's ears are usually long and mobile, to help them stay alert to danger, and also help them to keep cool. Lop-eared rabbits have been bred to have long, droopy ears, which may be more likely to get infected. The Netherland Dwarf has small ears and the shape of their heads means they are prone to dental problems.

## Lagomorphs

Rabbits belong to a group of animals called 'lagomorphs'. This means 'hare-like'. Lagomorphs also include pikas and hares. Lagomorphs are plant-eaters (herbivores). In the wild they are hunted by other animals, which means they tend to stay underground during the day. They are most active in the early morning, late afternoon and overnight. In the wild, rabbits live in underground burrows called warrens that can be home to a group of 50 or more rabbits.

## Tail

Rabbits have a short tail, which is sometimes called a scut. When they run, it moves up and down, flashing the white underside as a signal to other rabbits in the group to run, too.

## Legs

Rabbits have long, powerful back legs. Usually rabbits move with slow, hopping movements, but they can run at speeds of up to 50 miles per hour in short bursts to escape danger. If rabbits are chased, they run quickly, darting about in different directions to confuse predators.

## Digestion

Rabbits have an unusual way of digesting food. It passes through the gut and emerges as special droppings called 'caecotrophs'. These are then eaten, directly from their bottom, which allows the food to be reingested. Caecotrophs are dietary essentials for a rabbit to get all of the nutrients they need before any waste matter is passed as hard, pellet-like droppings.

## Feet

Like wild rabbits, domestic rabbits like to dig – using their front limbs to move the earth and the back ones to throw it backwards. Pet rabbits should be given the opportunity to perform this natural behaviour – digging boxes can be provided to encourage this. This activity will also help their claws to wear down naturally. You should still check your rabbit's claws regularly to make sure they are not damaged or overgrown.

## Teeth

A rabbit's top front teeth are called 'incisors'. They grow incredibly quickly, at a rate of up to 3mm a week. Eating lots of grass and hay helps rabbits to wear down their teeth, which is important to keep them healthy. You must check their teeth at least once a week and, if you notice any problems, seek veterinary advice immediately.

# Environment

1

Rabbits need a spacious enclosure.

# A suitable place to live

Before you bring your rabbits home, make sure you have prepared a suitable, safe, secure, hazard-free place for them to live. Part of being a responsible pet owner is making sure that your rabbits' complex needs are met so they can live happy and healthy lives. Some things to consider:

## A good location

Rabbits need a spacious, escape-proof enclosure in a quiet, calm place. If your rabbits are living outdoors, make sure their shelter is raised off the ground to stop it getting damp. All areas of your rabbits' home need to be well-ventilated, dry and draught-free and they must be protected from predators and extremes of weather and temperature. Areas of shade should also be provided in the living enclosure.

## A home, not a hutch

Rabbits are very active animals, so a traditional small hutch will not give them the space and stimulating environment that they need in order to live a happy and healthy life. Keeping rabbits in a small hutch can cause health and behaviour problems; they need to live in a space where they have enough room to hop, jump, run, play, dig and graze on growing grass. They also need to be able to stand upright on their back legs without their ears touching the roof of the enclosure, and be able to stretch out ▶

LEFT: Rabbits are very active, so they need a spacious enclosure. ABOVE: Rabbits should have constant access to hiding places. BELOW RIGHT: Rabbits can live indoors, too.

fully, in any direction, when lying down. For more information about suitably-sized homes see www.rspca.org.uk/rabbits.

## A shelter and living enclosure

Your rabbits also need a shelter where they can rest, feel safe and escape to during extreme temperatures or in bad weather. Remember that rabbits are most active in the early morning, late afternoon and overnight. This is when they like to graze and be sociable, so permanently attaching their shelter to a spacious run enables them to freely access their exercise area whenever they like. If possible, do not secure your rabbits in their shelter unless it is absolutely necessary.

## Hiding places

The rabbit is a prey species, so your pets must be able to hide in a secure place away from the sight and smell of predators, such as foxes, cats, dogs, ferrets and birds of prey, and whenever they feel scared or threatened. They should have constant access to their hiding places and you should make sure there is at least one such area per pet. It is also best to provide a hiding place that is big enough for all your rabbits to snuggle up in together if they want to. Platforms are a great addition to their enclosure, as rabbits can use these to scan the area around and below them for threats. They also add interest to their environment. See page 31 for more about enrichments.

## Indoor rabbits

Some people prefer to keep their rabbits indoors as house pets. The decision on whether this is suitable for your rabbits depends on their temperaments, previous lifestyle and experience and whether they are able to adjust to living inside. Whether you choose a large, indoor pen or a room to house them in, you must ensure that your home is fully rabbit-proofed. Keep your pets away from dangerous parts of the house, such as the kitchen, and ensure wires and other potential dangers, such as some house plants, are kept well away from them.

There are some advantages to keeping your rabbits indoors. It may encourage a closer bond to develop between you and your pets. You will be able to keep a closer eye on them and be more aware of any changes in their behaviour that could indicate that they are unwell. Rabbits are intelligent animals and can be taught to respond to commands with clicker training and can be litter-trained.

Ideally house rabbits should have daily access to a secure outside enclosure that has a main shelter and hiding places where they can exercise, dig and graze on growing grass. If the rabbits do not have an outside enclosure, kiln-dried grass and growing grass in trays or pots can be provided to enable them to graze. A 'dig box' filled with earth or child-safe play sand should also be placed in their enclosure. For further information, go to www.rspca.org.uk/rabbits/environment.

## Suitable bedding

Rabbits need plenty of bedding that's safe to eat and will also keep them warm and comfortable. Line the bottom of their shelter with newspaper and a layer of dust-free, non-cedar wood shavings, topped with dust-free hay or shredded paper. In winter you will need to check that they have plenty of extra bedding to keep them warm and dry. Check their shelter regularly to ensure it is still weatherproof, as leaks or damp will quickly affect the health of your rabbits. In periods of cold weather, make sure that their drinking water does not freeze and their bedding remains dry – it could freeze too and this could make your rabbits very ill.

If the temperature drops very low, consider moving your rabbits' enclosure into a shed or an unused garage where there are no vehicle fumes. This should be rabbit-proofed, and any items that could be chewed must be removed. Provide your rabbits with lots of additional bedding to snuggle into during the winter months. Do not give them blankets as they may chew them, which could result in an intestinal blockage.

Your rabbits will still need the chance to exercise every day in winter. For more on winter care, go to: www.rspca.org.uk/rabbits/health.

## Toileting and cleaning

Rabbits need constant access to a suitable toileting area. This should be separate from where they sleep. Litter trays should be lined with non-glossy newspaper, hay or straw, shredded paper and/or natural wood or paper-based non-clumping, non-expanding cat litter.

Toys will give your rabbits mental and physical stimulation. BELOW: Give your rabbits plenty of cosy bedding. RIGHT: Add familiar-smelling bedding and toys to your pet carrier.

Provide a litter tray for each of your rabbits; ideally with one more in addition. A hay rack can be placed over the litter tray to encourage hay-eating. Toileting areas should be cleaned every day. The rest of your rabbits' home should be cleaned weekly or more frequently if it is excessively soiled, using non-toxic cleaning products. Make sure that their home is thoroughly dried and, to reduce stress, add a small amount of the used bedding back into the toilet area and shelter so that it smells familiar to your pets.

## Toys, exercise and activities

Rabbits are intelligent and need plenty of toys and activities to enrich their lives and stop them getting bored. As well as making sure your rabbits can exercise outside every day, you need to give them the opportunity to explore

and play. There are lots of different toys available that can provide your rabbits with opportunities for physical exercise and mental stimulation. Items such as paper bags with the handles removed, tunnels, cardboard boxes with holes in them and cardboard tubes stuffed with hay are perfect for keeping your rabbits amused. You should also provide a digging box. A large litter tray or sand pit filled with earth or child-friendly sand is ideal. Choose toys for your rabbits with care and check them regularly for signs of damage or wear and tear to avoid any chance of injury. For more on toys, see page 31.

## Transporting your rabbits

It is very important to think about how you will transport your rabbits safely when you are first bringing them home and when you take them to the vet for appointments throughout their lives. Travelling can be stressful for rabbits and should be kept to a minimum, ideally transporting them only when absolutely necessary. There are several ways in which you can make their journey more comfortable and ensure that they are safe in your vehicle.

Choose a robust pet carrier – a cardboard carrier is not a good idea because it can be chewed by your rabbits and can also disintegrate if it gets wet. Putting familiar-smelling items (such as bedding) in the carrier will reassure your rabbits while they are on the move. Rabbits that live together should be transported in the same carrier, so make sure that the one that you choose is large enough for all of them. Travelling together will ease the journey and also means that any unfamiliar scents in the carrier will be transferred to all your rabbits, which can avoid any problems on their return home and the need for pets to be reintroduced after a time apart.

Place your carrier on the seat sideways on and secure it with the seatbelt, or place it on the floor in the footwell behind the seat. Never put the carrier in direct sunlight or in the boot of a car. Rabbits do not tolerate heat well, so ensure your vehicle is kept cool and well ventilated. You should also make sure that your rabbits have plenty of fresh water and hay for the journey. It can get unbearably hot in a car on a sunny day, even when it is not that warm outside, so be aware of this when you are transporting your rabbits. Do not leave them alone in a vehicle, as the temperature can quickly soar to unbearable levels, which can be fatal.

When your rabbits are back home, put them in their enclosure and allow them to rest for a while without being disturbed. This is particularly important when they come home for the first time, so they can get used to their new surroundings. You can download an advice sheet on transporting rabbits from: www.rspca.org.uk/rabbits/ environment.

## Holidays

When you go away on holiday, it is better that you find a responsible adult who can visit your pets and care for and meet all their welfare needs in their own home. If you are unable to do so, there are many boarding facilities that you can use. Use a reputable one that has been recommended to you. Visit it beforehand and question the owners/ staff about how they will care for your rabbits. You can help to settle in your rabbits by keeping them together and ensuring that they have familiar-smelling items, such as toys and some of their bedding, with them.

Diet

2

Your rabbits need access to clean, fresh water at all times.

# What to feed your rabbits

## A healthy diet

To stay fit and healthy, your rabbits need a well-balanced diet and constant access to fresh, clean water, which should be checked twice a day. Ensure water is algae-free in summer and doesn't freeze in winter. How much an individual rabbit needs to eat depends on their age, lifestyle and general health. If you have any concerns or queries about feeding, your vet will be able to give you detailed advice on what, and how much, to feed your rabbits.

## Bowls and bottles

Before you bring your rabbits home, you will need to buy a bottle or bowl for drinking water. Find out how your rabbits' water was offered to them in their previous home and use the same method. You should choose a good-quality drip-feed bottle, but do be aware that many rabbits prefer to drink from a bowl. If using bottles, check daily that rabbits can access the water and the end of the pipe is not blocked. In the wild, rabbits forage for food, so encourage this natural ▶

behaviour by scattering their food in their home. This will also keep them busy. For more on making mealtimes fun, see page 25. If you do buy food and water bowls, use heavy ceramic bowls which cannot be knocked over. Plastic bowls should be avoided, as they can be tipped over or chewed.

If you choose to use a food bowl, make sure it is suitably sized for your rabbits. If it is too big it is easy to overfill. Overfeeding your rabbits in this way can lead to weight gain and health issues. Make sure that your rabbits' food and water bowls (or bottle) are kept clean by washing them every day. Remove any uneaten food from the enclosure to stop it spoiling, but make sure they always have fresh hay available.

## The first few days

Usually a breeder or rescue centre will provide detailed information about what type of food your rabbits have been eating and their feeding routine. Ideally, a breeder should provide you with a week's supply of food for each rabbit when you collect them. Whenever possible, follow the feeding notes you have been given while your new rabbits are settling in, and stick to the type of food and routine they are used to. Any changes in a rabbit's diet should only be made gradually, as a sudden swap in brand or type of food can lead to them becoming very ill. If you have any concerns or queries about feeding, your vet will be able to give you detailed advice on what, and how much, to feed your rabbits.

## Grazing

Rabbits are grazers and they tend to eat for long periods, but mostly at dawn and dusk, so it is best to try to feed your rabbits during this period. In the wild, rabbits feed only on grass and other plants. A rabbit's digestive system needs hay and/or grass in order to work properly, so this should make up the majority of their diet. Grazing on hay and grass is also vital to keep a rabbit's teeth healthy and at the correct length and shape.

## Hay and greens

Good-quality hay and grass should make up the majority of your rabbits' diet and should be available at all times. Choose sweet-smelling hay that is dust-free and allow at least a rabbit-sized amount for each of your pets every day. Feeding rabbits the correct diet of mainly hay and/or grass will help prevent a lot of common diseases such as dental and gut disease. It is useful to think about getting a hay rack for your rabbits' enclosure. This will keep their food off the floor and stop the hay getting trampled and dirty. Placing the rack above their litter tray may encourage them to eat more hay. Find out which plants are safe to feed your rabbits. Offer your rabbits a variety of safe, washed leafy greens or weeds every day – ideally five or six different types. Safe plants include cabbage, kale, broccoli, parsley and mint. Don't feed them lawnmower clippings as these can upset their digestive system and make them ill.

## Nuggets

You can also give your rabbits a small, measured amount of good-quality commercial rabbit

nuggets, but these should not be a substitute for hay and grass, which must be available at all times. Always follow manufacturer's instructions when feeding nuggets. Choose nuggets that have high fibre levels. As a guide, you should allow around an egg-cup full per kilogram of body weight for each of your rabbits, but you should adjust the amount according to each pet's individual needs, based on their lifestyle, activity levels, age and state of health. Make sure your rabbits have finished the whole portion before you give them more; do not keep topping up the bowl, as this may result in them not eating enough hay and grass.

## Muesli-style foods

Muesli-style foods are associated with health problems in rabbits and should not be given to your pets. Feeding muesli can increase the risk of rabbits developing serious teeth and tummy problems, as well as obesity. These long-term health issues can cause your pets a lot of unnecessary suffering, which can be avoided if they are fed a balanced diet. You can find out more about this at: www.rspca. org.uk/rabbits/muesli.

If you currently feed your rabbits muesli, change their diet to a healthier one that ▶

TOP LEFT: Rabbits need safe, washed leafy greens every day. LEFT: RSPCA Healthy Nuggets for Adult Rabbits.

Give nuggets as part of your rabbits' daily diet.

is based on hay, grass, greens and nuggets. This transition should be done very gradually over several weeks, with detailed advice from your vet, to avoid making your rabbits ill.

## Treats

A rabbit's diet doesn't naturally include cereals, root vegetables or fruit, but you can give apples or root vegetables, like carrots, in small amounts as an occasional treat. Avoid feeding any other treats as these may harm your rabbits.

## New foods

Not all green leafy plants are safe to feed to your rabbits and some can be extremely poisonous. Your vet can advise you on what is safe, but if you are in any doubt, leave it out! Don't make any sudden changes to your rabbits' diet as this could make them very ill. Introduce new foods and make any changes gradually to avoid upsetting their digestive system. If you see any signs of an upset stomach, such as loose droppings, it is best to avoid that particular food and ask your vet for advice.

## Eating droppings (caecotrophy)

Rabbits produce two types of droppings. You may see a rabbit eating softer droppings – caecotrophs – directly from their bottom. Eating these is an essential part of a rabbit's diet because it helps them to get as much goodness as possible from their food. Your rabbit will also produce waste in the form of hard droppings.

## Weight watch

It is a good idea to note your rabbits' weight regularly and keep a careful eye on it. Remember that the majority of your pets' diet should be made up by hay and/or grass. You can help your rabbits to maintain a healthy weight by limiting treats – especially sweet ones such as apple and carrot – and ensuring that they are not over-fed on nuggets. Monitor your rabbits' weight and, if necessary, adjust the amount that you are feeding them. It is important to remember that young rabbits and pregnant and nursing females will have different needs to other rabbits. Ask your vet for advice on how to give them a balanced diet and if you need to adjust their food to help them to achieve a healthy weight.

## Changes in habits

Take note of the amount each of your rabbits eats and drinks every day, and watch out for any changes in an individual's eating, drinking or toileting habits. Check they are eating every day and that they are passing plenty of dry droppings. For example, if there is a reduction in the amount of droppings, or they stop, or if there are soft droppings sticking to their back end, talk to your vet straight away, as they could be ill.

## Things to avoid

Be aware that, as well as lawnmower clippings, there are many wild plants such as bindweed, poppies and buttercups that can also make your rabbits very ill. There is more on poisonous substances on page 43. If you are not sure whether a plant is safe for your rabbits, do not give it to them, as it may be toxic. If you think your rabbits may have eaten something poisonous, speak to your vet immediately.

Make mealtimes fun for your rabbits.

## MAKING MEALS FUN

There are many ways in which you can make your rabbits' mealtimes fun. In the wild, rabbits forage for food, so you can encourage this natural behaviour by scattering their greens and daily ration of nuggets around their home. Chewing can be encouraged by using wooden chew sticks designed for rabbits, or by giving them branches from fruit trees that have not been treated with chemicals.

You can also encourage natural behaviour by hanging greens so that your rabbits have to reach up while standing on their back legs to nibble them. Try hiding food in cardboard boxes or tubes for them to discover, too. Alternatively, you could fill puzzle feeders and balls with nuggets to add variety to their mealtimes. Do make sure, however, that there are enough feeders for each of your rabbits.

# Behaviour

3

Rabbits need plenty of space to exercise.

# Rabbit behaviour

Rabbits are very social animals and enjoy interacting with other friendly rabbits and people. They are also extremely active and require permanent access to a large enclosure so they can behave normally – running, hopping, jumping, playing, digging, grazing and stretching out. Rabbits are very playful, inquisitive animals and should have plenty of toys and activities to engage them, as well as being able to access all the things they need at all times, such as safe hiding places, food and water.

## Staying fit and healthy

By permanently attaching your rabbits' shelter (which could be a large hutch, cage, shed or playhouse) to a spacious enclosure, your rabbits will have complete freedom of movement so they can be active whenever they want. Your rabbits should have access to the main enclosure at all times, unless it is absolutely necessary to secure them in their shelter. Rabbits are most active in the early morning, late afternoon and overnight. This is when they like to graze, forage for food and be sociable, so you should try to make sure they are able to use a large area to move around in at these times in particular. Make sure that your rabbits have an interesting environment, in which there is plenty to do. This will give your rabbits plenty of mental and physical stimulation, which means that they are more likely to remain fit, healthy and happy as a result.

## Being social

In the wild, rabbits live in social groups that can include 50 or more individuals. Because of this, it is essential that your pets are able to interact with other friendly rabbits, unless advised otherwise by a vet or qualified animal behaviourist. Rabbits should not be kept alone and should also not be paired with guinea pigs. Their needs are completely different and rabbits can bully or injure the guinea pig.

Some rabbits may enjoy learning new skills through positive reward-based training – you can find out more about this on page 35.

## Hiding places

Rabbits are prey for animals such as cats, dogs, foxes, ferrets and birds of prey, so they need to have plenty of places to escape to if they feel scared or threatened, where they can hide out of the sight and smell of a predator.

It is essential that you provide enough hiding places for each of your rabbits, plus one that is large enough for them all to hide in together. These should be in addition to the main shelter. Hiding places should be positioned in a quiet area, away from draughts and direct sunlight. They should be large enough for a rabbit to move swiftly underneath, but still low enough to give them a sense of security. Hiding places should have two exits to prevent a dominant rabbit becoming territorial or aggressive to others inside. If you keep different-sized

ABOVE: Rabbits need space and a stimulating environment. RIGHT: Platforms add variety and can act as a 'look-out' point.

rabbits together you should also make sure that the smaller rabbit has a hiding place with entrances that the larger rabbit cannot fit through, so they can escape from their larger companion if they want to.

For your rabbits to feel that their hiding places remain safe and secure it is extremely important that you do not remove them from it, or trap them inside.

## Platforms

Platforms allow rabbits to scan their environment for threats and can help them to feel safe. Jumping on and off the platform will also help to build a rabbit's physical fitness and bone strength. If any of your rabbits have previously been kept in a restricted environment, with little or no opportunity to exercise and jump onto objects, check with your vet to make

sure that platforms are suitable for them. You can find out more about providing platforms at: www.rspca.org.uk/rabbits/platforms.

## Digging

Many rabbits love to dig, so try to give them some sort of 'digging box'. This could be a large plant pot or litter tray filled with earth, a cardboard box filled with shredded paper or a sandpit filled with child-friendly sand. The digging box should be a safe place for them to have fun.

## Scent marking

Scent is a very important form of communication for rabbits. They mark their territory using chin secretions, urine and droppings. 'Chin-marking', or 'chin-rubbing', is performed by the rabbits rubbing their chins on an object or part of their enclosure. This transfers secretions from their scent gland onto the item. Rabbits mark their territory, making it smell familiar and reassuring, but these scents are not detected by people. This is why it is important when you are cleaning your rabbits' home to make sure that you return some of the old bedding to the enclosure, so that it still smells familiar and safe to them. Where possible, if a rabbit needs to be removed from the enclosure to travel, such as to the vet for a health check-up, it is best to transport them with their companions so that scents are shared and remain familiar. This helps to avoid potential problems associated with reintroducing rabbits to one another after time apart.

## When there are problems

Every rabbit is different and the way in which they behave will depend upon their age as well as personality and experiences. It is important to make sure that you are very familiar with your rabbits' normal behaviour and routine. If a rabbit's behaviour changes, this could be a sign that they are frightened, bored, ill or in pain. These signs may include differences in eating or toileting habits, hiding, being aggressive, chewing their enclosure, overgrooming, playing with their water bottle, circling the enclosure, sitting hunched or being reluctant to move. If you see any alterations in the behaviour of any of your rabbits, consult your vet so they can give your pets a check-up and rule out any illnesses or injury that could be causing the issue. Your vet may refer you to an animal behaviourist for advice. You can find links to information about animal behaviourists on page 46, or by going to: www.rspca.org.uk/findabehaviourist.

Never shout at or punish your rabbits; they are very unlikely to understand and may become nervous or scared. If your rabbit's behaviour develops into an ongoing problem, talk to an expert.

# Toys

There are many inexpensive ways of enriching your rabbits' environment. Providing toys enables your pets to perform normal behaviours such as digging, chewing, chin-marking (see page 29) and investigating. You can experiment with different toys and swap them occasionally to prevent your rabbits getting bored. Bear in mind that routine is important for rabbits, though, so once you find things they enjoy, make sure their favourite toys are available at the same time of day to avoid distressing them.

When you introduce new toys or objects to your rabbits' environment, keep a close eye on your pets to make sure they are not stressed or frightened. Be sure that they can move away from or hide from the item. If they seem very frightened or stressed by the new toy, remove it and monitor their behaviour. Remember that you should not go toy mad! Do not fill your rabbits' enclosure with so many items that they can no longer exercise easily. As you get to know your rabbits, you will find that each will have a preference for different toys. It is important to make sure that there are enough items for

TOP RIGHT: Swap toys regularly to keep things interesting.
RIGHT: Tunnels and cardboard tubes make perfect toys.

**TUNNELS** You can purchase ones made of plastic or fabric. They can also be made from cardboard boxes, cardboard tubes and large ceramic pipes.

**OBJECTS TO MANIPULATE**
Untreated straw/wicker/seagrass mats and baskets, balls and plastic flowerpots are great for rabbits to investigate. Some solid plastic baby toys – such as 'key rings'/rattles/ stacking cups – and robust cat and parrot toys can be great for rabbits. Ensure there are no small parts that could be swallowed and supervise their use. If you can, try hiding some of your rabbits' food in or under these toys to encourage them to forage. For more toy ideas that your rabbits may enjoy, go to: www.rspca.org.uk/rabbits/toys.

each rabbit. This will avoid competition and a situation in which one rabbit monopolizes a particular item.

Here are some toy ideas to try with your rabbits:

**PAPER** Shredded newspaper, paper bags with the handles removed and telephone directories (with the glossy covers removed). Bundle up your rabbits' favourite food item in brown paper as a parcel for them to discover.

**CARDBOARD BOXES** with holes cut into them make great hiding places. Cardboard tubes can be stuffed with hay and healthy treats as part of their daily food allowance and can encourage your rabbits to explore.

**SAFETY FIRST** Make sure anything you give your rabbits is safe and appropriate. Materials should be non-toxic with smooth, rounded edges. Inspect toys regularly and discard any that are damaged or dangerous. Do not give them blankets, as rabbits have a tendency to chew them, which could result in an intestinal blockage.

Company

4

Rescue organizations can often pair suitable rabbits.

# Being with others

Rabbits are naturally sociable animals and normally prefer to live in pairs or in a group. A rabbit left alone without company and nothing to do may suffer and develop abnormal behaviours. So unless you have been specifically advised otherwise by a vet or qualified animal behaviourist, always house your rabbits in pairs or groups.

## A good mix

One of the reasons that people used to be concerned about keeping rabbits in pairs or groups was because of the risk of pregnancy. Now rabbits of both sexes are routinely neutered. A good combination of rabbits is a neutered male and a neutered female. Neutering rabbits not only reduces the risk of fighting in both males and females but can also have important health benefits for your pet. For more on neutering your rabbit, go to: www.rspca.org.uk/rabbits/health.

## Pecking order

Rabbits will naturally form a 'pecking order', with some animals being more dominant than others, which means that the non-dominant animals can sometimes be bullied by the dominant rabbit. This is another reason why it is important to make sure that all your rabbits have constant access to hiding places – and enough of them – so that they can get away from each other if they want to.

## Introducing new rabbits

Rabbits that are brought up together will usually get on with each other, but if they are introduced for the first time as adults they may fight. Introducing new rabbits should be a gradual process and must be done under close supervision – preferably in a space that is new to both rabbits. Always talk to a qualified animal behaviourist if you are unsure or have problems. If you are rehoming rescue rabbits, a rescue organization such as the RSPCA may be able to pair suitable rabbits for you.

## Rabbits and guinea pigs

The best companion for a rabbit is another friendly rabbit. Rabbits and guinea pigs have different needs, so keeping them together is not advised. For further information, including advice on what to do if you already have a rabbit and guinea pig living together, visit: www.rspca.org.uk/rabbitsandguineapigs.

## Other pets

Rabbits will usually be scared of cats and dogs because they are natural predators, but if introduced to them carefully, early in life, they can develop friendships. Never leave your rabbits unsupervised with a cat or dog, though, even if you know they are good friends.

## Rabbits and children

Many families with children keep rabbits. Having a pet can improve a child's social skills and caring for an animal can encourage kindness, understanding and responsibility. While children will quickly learn to treat new rabbits as part of the family, it is important to teach them to handle them gently and carefully. Always supervise your children when they are interacting with rabbits and minimize the risk of them accidentally dropping your pets by getting them to sit on the ground to pet or hold them. Only adults and responsible older children should be allowed to pick up rabbits, to reduce the risk of injury if the rabbit is mishandled or accidentally dropped.

## Safety first

Never leave your rabbits unsupervised with another animal or person who may deliberately or accidentally harm or frighten them. When you are away, make sure your rabbits are properly cared for by a responsible person who can give them the care and company they need.

If one of your rabbits shows any changes in behaviour or regular signs of stress or fear, such as hiding or aggression when they are being handled you should seek expert advice. It is important to get your rabbit checked by a vet first to rule out any form of illness or injury that could be causing their reaction. Your vet can then refer you to a behaviour expert.

## Training your rabbit

Rabbits are intelligent and training them is another great way to spend time together and enhance your bond. Rabbits can be taught a variety of tricks, which provides mental and physical stimulation. You can litter train your rabbits, as well as teach them various tricks such as coming when called, entering their shelter on cue, retrieving objects and even using a cat flap. Only positive reward-based methods such as clicker training should be used. Consulting a behaviour expert may be useful in learning how to train your rabbit effectively.

TOP LEFT: Rescue organizations can often pair suitable rabbits.

# You and your rabbits

A good relationship with your rabbit can be rewarding for both you and your pet, as well as making the process of catching and transporting your animal, taking your rabbit for routine veterinary examinations and carrying out health checks much easier. If for any reason your vet or qualified animal behaviourist has advised you that your pet has to be kept on their own, it is especially important that you interact positively with your rabbit every day to provide the companionship they need to stay happy and healthy.

**HANDLING YOUR RABBITS** Being a prey species, rabbits constantly look out for predators. A rabbit's natural response to a perceived threat is to flee. It is worth remembering that the only time a rabbit is picked up in the wild, apart from by their mother, is when they are captured by a predator, so learning to handle your rabbits correctly is vital to ensure they do not view you as a threat.

Your rabbit's reaction to handling is likely to depend on their past experiences. This is especially true of rabbits who are not used to being handled or have been handled roughly at one time in their life, as they may find human contact distressing. This response can be expressed as fearfulness, escape behaviour and aggression.

It is important to be patient when handling your rabbits; this will allow them to grow more confident and comfortable around you. To avoid startling your rabbits, always move slowly and talk quietly around them. Attempting to handle your rabbit from a standing position may scare them. Where possible, it is best if all interactions are carried out at ground level, as people are likely to be perceived as less threatening when in this position. Picking your rabbit up when you are positioned close to the ground is also likely to be less frightening for them and reduces the risk of injury if they are accidentally dropped.

With time and patience you can help your rabbit grow more confident and comfortable around people. If you are concerned about your rabbit's behaviour or about issues around handling your rabbit, ask your vet or a qualified animal behaviourist for advice.

To hold your rabbits correctly, pick them up gently but firmly, making sure that one hand supports their back and hindquarters at all times and that they feel secure by having all four feet held against your body. Covering your rabbit's eyes (with a towel or with the crook of you arm) can help them feel more relaxed, but make sure that their nostrils are not covered. Always be gentle and use the minimum effective level of restraint, according to the animal's temperament and health status. Never pick up your rabbit by the ears; this would be extremely stressful for them and is highly likely to result in injury to them.

For more detailed advice on how to handle your rabbits, go to: www.rspca.org.uk/rabbits/company.

TOP LEFT: It is best to interact with your rabbit at ground level. LEFT: How to hold your rabbit.

# Health
# and welfare

5

Speak to your vet immediately if you notice any changes in your rabbit's behaviour.

# Protecting your pet

Rabbits can suffer from a range of infectious diseases and other illnesses, especially dental disease. They can catch deadly diseases from wild rabbits, so you should prevent your pets having contact with wild rabbits or areas where they may have been living. Rabbits feel pain in the same way as other mammals, including people, but they are not very good at showing outward signs of pain and may be suffering a great deal before you notice anything is wrong. It is vital that you check your rabbits for signs of injury or illness every day, and make sure someone else does this if you are away. If you notice a change in the way one of your rabbits behaves, a loss of appetite, or if they are unusually quiet, this can be a sign that your pet is ill or in pain. Talk to your vet immediately.

## Find a vet and arrange insurance

It is important to find a vet with whom you can register your new rabbits and book them in for a check-up and ▶

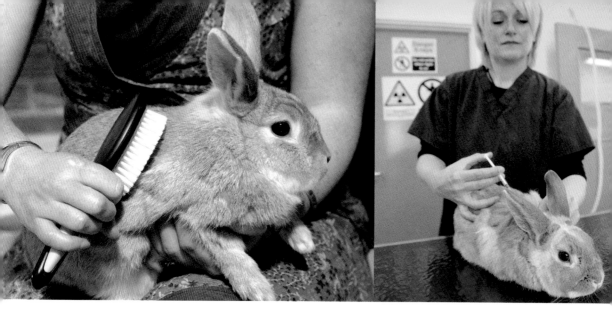

◀ vaccinations. The vet will be able to give you lots of information about looking after your rabbits, neutering them and other detailed pet-care advice. You can read more about finding a vet and low-cost vet care at www.rspca.org.uk/whatwedo/vetcare.

Check the insurance situation, too. Some charities and breeders may provide a short period of insurance cover which you can either take over and extend, or you may want to arrange an alternative policy. Where this is not provided, it is a good idea to arrange for an insurance policy to start from the moment you pick up your rabbits.

## Vaccinations

Vaccinations are very important for rabbits to prevent certain deadly diseases such as myxomatosis and Rabbit Haemorrhagic Disease (RHD), which is also known as VHD. It is essential that you vaccinate your rabbits, whether they live outdoors or indoors, against both myxomatosis and RHD. If your rabbits

have already been vaccinated the vet will have given them a vaccination certificate which shows the date on which it was administered and the products used. For more information go to: www.rspca.org. uk/rabbits/vaccinations.

## Health checks

Take your rabbits for a routine health check with your vet at least once a year. It is a good chance to ask for advice about things you can do to protect your rabbits' health, such as essential vaccinations.

## Worms

Worms may be visible in faeces or around the rabbit's rear end area. Speak to your vet immediately if you notice any sign of worms. It is important to keep your rabbits' enclosure clean by removing droppings and rotating the areas they have access to. You should also disinfect food and water containers, as well as their housing, using a cleaner that is safe for animals.

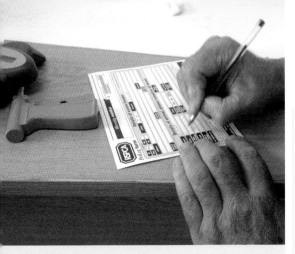

LEFT TO RIGHT: Groom your rabbits regularly. Vaccinating your rabbits will protect them from several diseases. Microchip your rabbit.

## IN AN EMERGENCY

**Emergencies can be really scary, but try not to panic.**

**1** **If you think your rabbits are ill or injured, stay calm.**

**2** **Contact your vet for advice immediately – always phone before taking your rabbits in as they may be able to give you essential advice over the phone, or you may need to go to a different place than normal.**

**3** **Follow your vet's advice. If you are advised to take your rabbits to the vet, do so quickly and calmly.**

**Only give your rabbits medicines that have been specifically recommended for that animal by a vet – some medicines used for other animals can be very dangerous to rabbits.**

## Microchipping

Microchipping your rabbits gives them the best chance of being identified and returned to you if they are lost or stolen. A tiny microchip containing a unique code is inserted under their skin. This can be scanned and matched to your details, which are held on a database, so make sure you keep your contact information up to date.

## Grooming

Your rabbits should be brushed regularly with a grooming brush or soft baby's hairbrush to keep their fur in good condition. Long-haired rabbits will need to be groomed every day to prevent their fur getting dirty and matted. If you are unsure how to groom your rabbits properly, ask your vet for advice.

## Teeth and nails

A rabbit's nails and front teeth should be checked at least once a week as these can grow quickly. Rabbits' teeth grow continuously throughout their life and need to be worn down and kept at the correct length and shape by chewing on grass, hay and leafy green plants – if rabbits don't eat the right sorts of food they can suffer from serious dental disease. If your rabbit's teeth are overgrown or misaligned, or their claws are long or damaged, your vet will be able to deal with them.

# Health issues

**FLYSTRIKE** Flystrike happens when flies lay their eggs in the fur of animals, particularly around their bottoms. The maggots hatch and eat their way into rabbits' skin. Flystrike can occur in hours; toxic shock and death can result very quickly. Speak to your vet immediately if an animal becomes infested. Make sure that you clean your rabbits' toilet areas every day, do the same to their housing and change their bedding at least once a week. In warm weather check the fur and skin around your rabbits' rear ends and tail areas twice a day, as urine staining or droppings that are stuck will attract flies. If your pet's back end is dirty, clean it immediately with warm water and ensure the area is dried thoroughly. Speak to your vet about the best way of reducing the risk of flystrike before warmer weather starts. (See www.rspca.org.uk/adviceandwelfare/pets/general/flystrike.)

**COCCIDIOSIS** The parasite responsible for coccidiosis is passed from an infected rabbit via their droppings. Young kits are especially vulnerable around weaning time. Some infected rabbits will not have symptoms, but others may have diarrhoea, weight loss or loss of appetite and become weak. If you notice any of these symptoms, speak to your vet immediately. Good hygiene, such as keeping your rabbits' enclosure clean and keeping their food off the floor, can help to reduce the chances of them contracting this disease.

***ENCEPHALITOZOONCUNICULI (E. CUNICULI)*** This condition is caused by a parasite. Other rabbits can pick up the parasite from the urine of an infected rabbit, most probably when it gets onto food or water. Kits can be infected during pregnancy. E. cuniculi can cause many symptoms, including lack of coordination, eye problems, weight loss and increased thirst. If you notice any of these symptoms or any change in your rabbits' behaviour, talk to your vet immediately. Cleaning your rabbits' home, bowls and bottles can help to kill off the parasites.

**CONSTIPATION AND DIARRHOEA** If you notice a

rabbit's eating or drinking habits have changed, the quantity of their droppings reduces or stops or they have loose droppings, ask your vet for advice immediately – they could be seriously ill.

**PNEUMONIA** Damp hutches and bedding can leave rabbits at risk of pneumonia. If you notice one of your rabbits has laboured breathing, loss of appetite or a discharge coming from its nose, speak to your vet immediately.

**SNUFFLES** This is a highly infectious disease that is similar to the human common cold. It can also lead to pneumonia. If you notice one of your rabbits is sneezing and that they have running eyes or nose, or wet front paws from wiping a running nose, take them to your vet for treatment.

**STRESS** Rabbits that are stressed are much more likely to become ill, so try to minimize unnecessary stress, provide constant access to safe hiding places and establish a predictable routine. Keep a close eye on your rabbits' behaviour, eating and drinking habits and droppings. If anything changes or they are showing signs of fear or stress, seek advice from your vet or a qualified animal behaviourist.

**POISONING** The poisoning of a pet is every responsible owner's nightmare. Make sure you are prepared for such an emergency. Preventing your rabbits coming into contact with poisonous substances and treating any accidental poisonings quickly and appropriately is an important part of responsible pet ownership. Common items that are poisonous to rabbits include: rodent poisons – also known as 'rodenticides' – ivy, rhubarb, foxgloves and glyphosate herbicide products. Never give your rabbits greens picked from the side of the road, as they may have been sprayed with pesticides that could be fatal to them.

If you suspect your pet has been poisoned, act fast and contact your vet for advice immediately. Signs of poisoning include diarrhoea, dehydration, loss of appetite, lethargy, abnormal heart rhythm and tremors. For more detailed advice on preventing and dealing with poisoning, go to: www.rspca.org.uk/poisoning.

# Your questions answered

*Dr Jane Tyson BSc (Hons) MSc PhD, rabbit behaviour and welfare expert, Companion Animals Department, RSPCA*

**Q: What do I need to know about rabbits' health before I buy them?**
**A:** Before you make the final decision to buy or rehome rabbits make sure you ask plenty of questions; for example, find out what they have been fed and how they have been cared for. Some breeds of rabbit have been selected for exaggerated physical features that can cause them to suffer and

reduce their quality of life, while certain breeds are particularly prone to inherited disorders and diseases. These can lead to costly vet bills. Find out if the rabbits have shown any signs of behavioural problems, too. If you are unsure about anything, ask a vet for advice before you commit to taking on a rabbit, and if you are still not happy, it is better to look elsewhere.

**Q: My new rabbits are very timid and hate being picked up. How can I help them?**
**A:** It is important to give your rabbits plenty of time to adjust and settle into their new home. Be quiet, positive and gentle when you are interacting with them. There are more tips on this on page 36. Remember that your rabbits may not be used to being handled, so you will need to take things very slowly and gently to allow them to get used to interacting with you. It is also a good idea to get them checked by your vet to rule out any illness or injury that could be causing the problem. Your vet can give you advice and, if they feel it is necessary, they may

refer you to a qualified animal behaviourist. A behaviourist will work to identify the cause of the problem and help your rabbits to get used to being handled. Find out more at www.rspca.org.uk/findabehaviourist.

**Q: My rabbits are scratching. Could they have fleas?**
**A:** Rabbits can suffer from several external parasites including lice, ticks, mites and fleas – all of which can make your rabbit scratch. Parasites can also transmit diseases; for example, fleas can carry myxomatosis. Check your rabbits' fur regularly and carefully – you may see insects crawling about, or eggs or dark specks. Ticks attach themselves to rabbits and feed on their blood for several days. If your rabbits scratch or rub their ears or shake their head they may have ear mites. If you notice any signs of parasites you should contact your vet immediately. They will advise on the best treatment. If you have a variety of animals you must use the appropriate treatments for each, as advised by your vet.

**Q: We're going on holiday soon. Is it best to use a boarding service or to arrange for my rabbits to be cared for at home?**

**A:** Transporting rabbits is stressful for them, so try to find someone to care for and meet all your rabbits' welfare needs within their familiar home. If you are boarding your rabbits, try to make the move less stressful by keeping pairs/groups together and leave them with familiar-smelling items, such as toys. You can find more on holidays at www.rspca.org.uk/holiday.

FAR LEFT: Ask plenty of questions to make sure you are buying or rehoming a happy, healthy rabbit LEFT: Check your rabbits for signs of external parasites such as mites and fleas.

# Index

abdomen, 11
age, 6
aggression, 30, 35, 36
Angoras, 9
Animal Welfare Act, 5
appetite, loss of, 39, 43
apples, 24, 25
Argentes, 8
Astrex, 9

bedding, 17, 29, 42
behaviour changes, 25, 30, 35, 39, 42, 43
Beveren, 8
biology, 4, 12–13
blankets, 31
bottles/bowls, 21–2
breathing difficulties, 11, 42

caecotrophy (eating droppings), 13, 24
cardboard boxes, 18, 29, 31
carriers, 19
carrots, 24, 25
chew sticks, 25
children, 35
Chinchilla, 8
chin-marking/rubbing, 29
choosing/buying a rabbit, 6–7, 10–11, 34, 44
claws, 11, 41
coccidiosis, 43
colour, 9
company, 28, 33–5
constipation, 42
crossbreeds, 7

Dalmatian, 8
dental problems, 12, 39
diarrhoea, 11, 24, 42, 43

digestion, 13
digestive complaints, 23, 24
digging boxes, 13, 18, 29
droppings, 24, 25, 29, 42

ears, 11, 12, 37
emergencies, 41
Encephalitozoon cuniculi, 42
enclosures/shelter, 15–16, 27, 28
exaggerated features, 12, 44
exercise, 5, 18, 27, 28–9
eyes, 5, 11

fancy breeds, 9
feeding, 21–5
feet, 13
fleas/ticks, 45
Flemish Giant, 9
flystrike, 42
fur breeds, 8

gestation, 5
glyphosate, 43
grazing, 22–3
grooming, 5, 41
guinea pigs, 5, 9, 28, 35

handling, 36–7, 44
Harlequin, 9
hay/grass, 22–3
health/welfare, 4–5, 11, 39–43
hiding places, 16, 28, 34, 43
Himalayan, 9
holidays, 19, 45
hutch, 5, 15, 27
hygiene, 17–18, 40, 41, 42, 43

indoors, keeping rabbits, 16–17
information, 11
insurance, 4, 40

keeping alone, 28, 33

lagomorphs, 12
lawnmower clippings, 23, 25
legs, 13
lethargy, 11, 43
life expectancy, 4, 5
litter size, 5
litter trays, 17–18

medicine, giving, 41
microchipping, 41
mites, 45
muesli-style food, 23–4
myxomatosis, 40, 45

nails, 41
Netherland Dwarf, 12
neutering, 5, 6, 7, 34, 40
nose, 11
nuggets, 23

obesity, 22, 23

paper, 17, 29, 31
parasites, 42, 43
pecking order, 34
pets, rabbits with other, 35
platforms, 28–9
play, 18, 31–2
pneumonia, 42
poisoning, 43
poisonous plants, 25
pregnancy, 7, 25, 29, 34, 42
puberty, 5
purebreds, 7

Rabbit Haemorrhagic Disease (RHD/VHD), 40
rabbit sizes, 7

# Resources

rabbit types, 8–9
rescue rabbits, 34
Rex, 8–9
rodenticides, 43

safety, 31, 35
scent marking, 29
sex, 6
Siberian, 8
Silver Fox, 8
skin conditions, 11
snuffles, 42–3
stress, 19, 36, 37, 43
stimulation, 25, 27, 35

tail, 12
teeth, 11, 13, 41
toileting, 17–18
toys, 18, 30–1
training, 28, 35
transporting, 18–19, 29, 45
treats, 24
tunnels, 31

urine, 29, 42

vaccinations, 11, 40
veterinary care, 5, 39–40

water, 5, 17, 19, 21
water bottles, 21–2, 30, 40
weaning, 5
weight, 5
weight issues, 22, 23
weight watching, 24–5
worms, 40

## RSPCA

For more information and advice from the RSPCA about caring for your rabbit, go to www.rspca.org.uk/rabbits.

## Veterinary advice

- Find a vet: Advice on finding low-cost veterinary care at www.rspca.org.uk/findavet

- Vet Help Direct at www.vethelpdirect.com.

- Vetfone: www.vetfone.co.uk. (24-hour service)

- Find a Vet at www.findavet.rcvs.org.uk/home.

## Behaviour advice

- Advice on finding a behaviourist at www.rspca.org.uk/findabehaviourist.

- The Association for the Study of Animal Behaviour (ASAB) at www.asab.org.

- The Association of Pet Behaviour Counsellors (APBC) at www.apbc.org.uk.

- If you are concerned about your rabbits' behaviour, contact a major rescue organization or rehoming centre, such as the RSPCA, for expert advice. They will be happy to help you, even if you have not adopted your pet from their rehoming centres.

## Other resources

- The website www.rabbitawarenessweek.co.uk has lots of useful information and advice on caring for rabbits.

PET GUIDE

# Learn more about other popular pets with these bestselling RSPCA pet guides

RSPCA
PET GUIDE

**Care for Your Guinea Pigs**

Find out what your guinea pigs need to stay happy and healthy

RSPCA
PET GUIDE

**Care for Your Hamster**

Find out what your hamster needs to stay happy and healthy

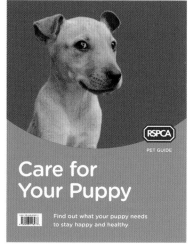

RSPCA
PET GUIDE

**Care for Your Puppy**

Find out what your puppy needs to stay happy and healthy

RSPCA
PET GUIDE

**Care for Your Kitten**

Find out what your kitten needs to stay happy and healthy